1·2·3 Draw

DINOSAURS

and other prehistoric animals

by

Freddie Levin

Peel Productions, Inc.

Before you begin

You will need:

1. a pencil
2. an eraser
3. a pencil sharpener
4. lots of paper (recycle and re-use!)
5. colored pencils
6. a folder for saving work
7. a comfortable place to draw
8. good light

Now let's begin...!

Published by Peel Productions, Inc.
Printed in China.

Cataloging-in-Publication Data
Levin, Freddie.
    1-2-3 draw dinosaurs and other prehistoric animals /
    by Freddie Levin. p. cm.
    Includes index.
    ISBN 0-939217-41 -4 (pbk.)
    1. Dinosaurs in art--Juvenile literature. 2. Drawing--
    Technique--Juvenile literature. I. Title: One-two-three
    draw dinosaurs and other prehistoric animals. II. Title.

NC780.5 .L48 2000
743.6--dc21   00-057450

Distributed to the trade and art
markets in North America by

NORTH LIGHT BOOKS,
an imprint of F&W Publications, Inc.
4700 East Galbraith Road
Cincinnati, OH 45236

(800) 289-0963

Contents

Important drawing tip number 1:
*** Draw lightly at first, so you can erase extra lines. ***

Important drawing tip number 2:
*** Have fun drawing dinosaurs and other prehistoric animals! ***

Important drawing tip number 3:
*** Practice, practice, practice and you will get better! ***

Circles, Ovals and Eggs

The drawings in this book start with three basic shapes:

circle   **oval**   **egg**

*A circle is perfectly round.

*An oval is a squashed circle.

*An egg is an oval with one side fatter than the other.

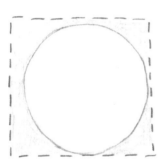 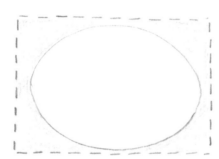 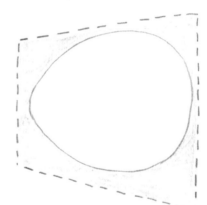

A **circle**
fits inside
a square.

An **oval**
fits inside
a rectangle.

An **egg**
fits inside
a trapezoid.

The more you practice drawing **circles,**
ovals and **eggs,** the easier it will be.

Remember:

Draw lightly!

Note to parents and teachers:
I have found it helpful in working
with very young children with
poorly developed motor control to
have them begin their drawings
by tracing a small cardboard
cutout of an egg, oval, or circle.

What Color Were the Dinosaurs?

All the animals in this book are extinct. That means they died out long ago. Now we know them only from their bones. People who study these fossil bones are called paleontologists. Paleontologists can tell the appearance of dinosaurs and other animals by the shape of their bones.

We can only guess at their colors and markings. After all, who would know about a zebra's spectacular stripes from looking just at its bones? The reptile, bird and animal worlds have many colorful members.

So, have fun. Make your dinosaurs any color you want. I did!

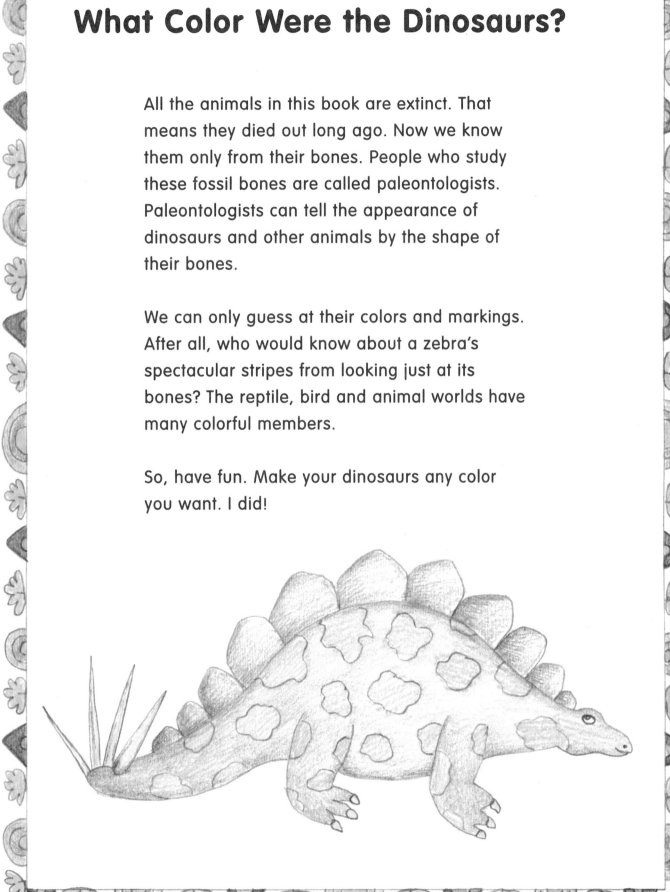

Deinonychus

(dye - NON - ik - us)

Deinonychus means "terrible claw." It was small (11 feet long) and fast, and had good eyesight. It was named for the gigantic claw on its rear foot. Deinonychus hunted in packs. Its favorite food was meat.

1 Start with two **eggs**, one larger than the other.

2 Draw the neck. Shape the face. Draw a long pointy tail.

3 Add an eye and nose. Draw the mouth. Draw two front legs and feet. Draw back legs in sections. Add feet.

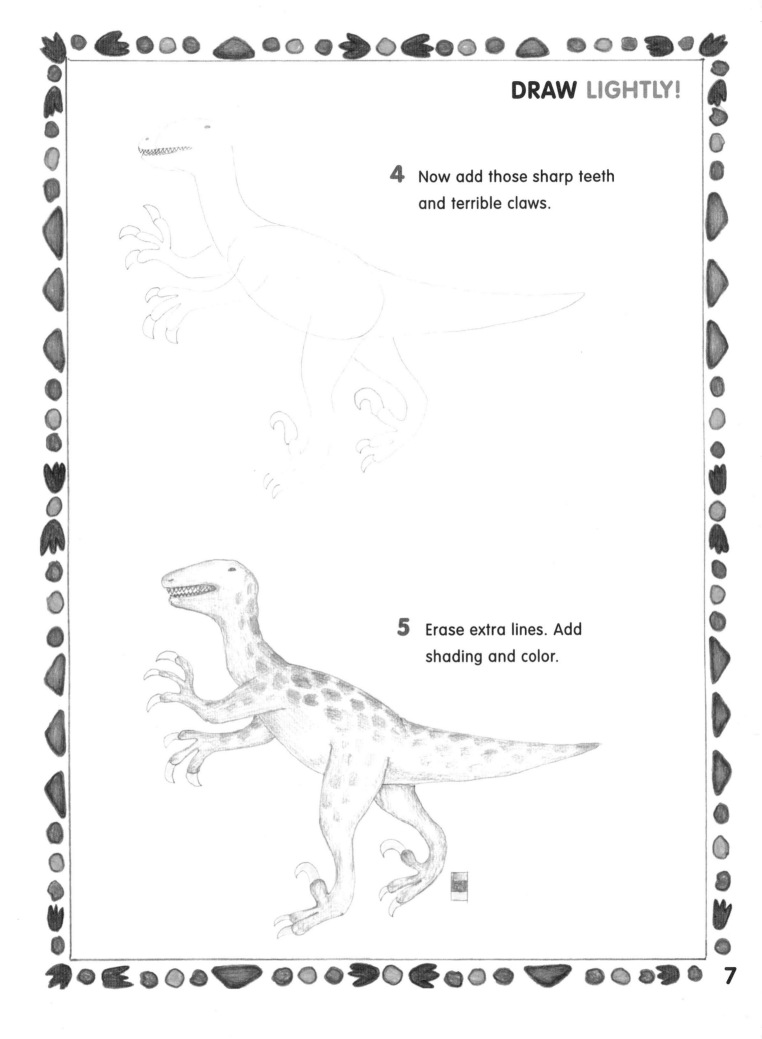

4 Now add those sharp teeth and terrible claws.

5 Erase extra lines. Add shading and color.

Iguanodon

(ee - GWAN - oh - don)

Iguanodon means "iguana tooth." One of the first fossils ever found, it was thought the tooth looked like that of the modern iguana. Big as an elephant and equipped with thumb spikes, Iguanodon was a forest-dwelling plant eater.

1 Start with a **circle** and an **egg**.

2 Shape the face. Make a line for the mouth. Add a curved neck. Draw the tail.

3 Add an eye and a nostril. Draw a front leg and rear leg.

4 Add another front leg.
Draw thumb spikes on
each front leg. Draw
another back leg.

5 Erase extra lines.
Add shading and color.

Stegosaurus

(steg - oh - SORE - us)

Tiny-brained Stegosaurus was 25 feet long, 11 1/2 feet high and weighed 2 tons. A plant eater, the bony plates and tail spikes were probably for protection.

1 Start with a large **oval** and a small **oval**. Notice the angle of the ovals.

2 Draw a curving tail. Shape the face and add an eye and nostril.

3 Add the bony plates all along the back. Notice that the ones in the middle are bigger. Draw two legs and feet.

4 Draw tail spikes. Add toenails.

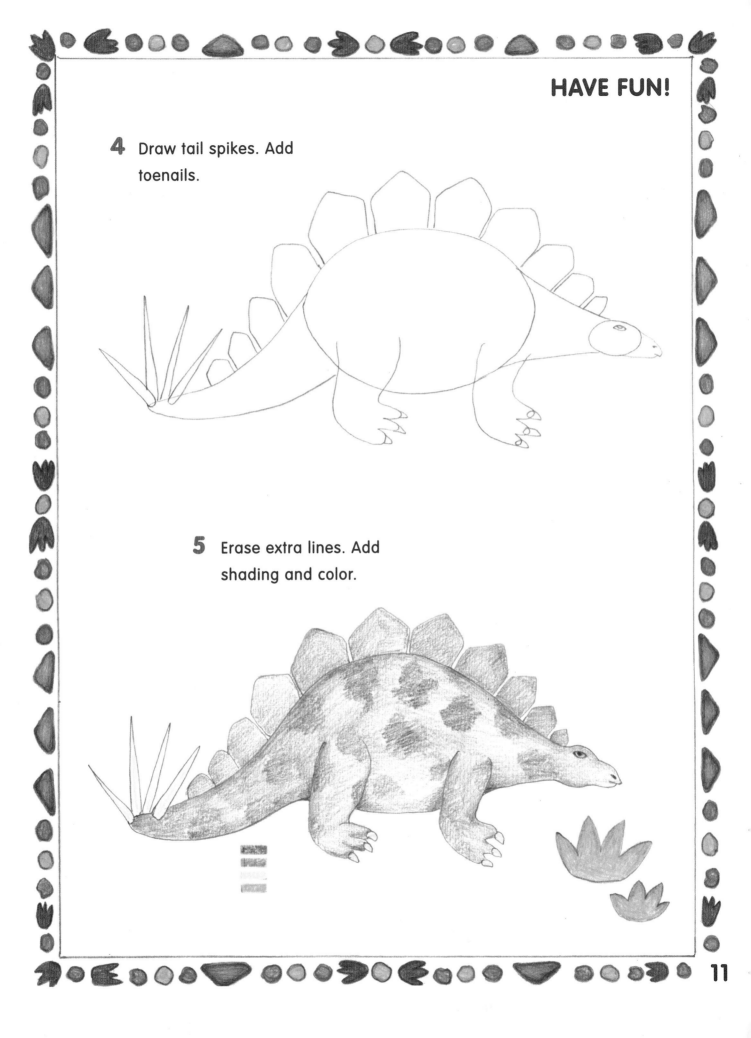

5 Erase extra lines. Add shading and color.

Tyrannosaurus

(ty - ran - oh -SORE -us)

One of the best-known dinosaurs, this meat-eating terror had 6" long razor-sharp teeth and stood 40 feet tall. Some scientists believe that Tyrannosaurus was not a hunter but a scavenger who ate prey already dead.

1   Start with a medium-sized **egg** and a large **oval**.

2   Add a mouth, nostril, and eye. Draw a curved neck. Add two front limbs. Draw four "U" shapes for the back legs.

3 Draw sharp teeth, and add the eyebrow. Draw the long tail. Add the two feet and sharp claws.

4 Erase extra lines. Add shading and color.

Tyriffic Tyrannosaurus!

Ankylosaurus
(an - KY - low - sore - us)

Ankylosaurus means "stiff lizard." It had bony plates and tail spikes for protection. Ankylosaurus was a plant eater.

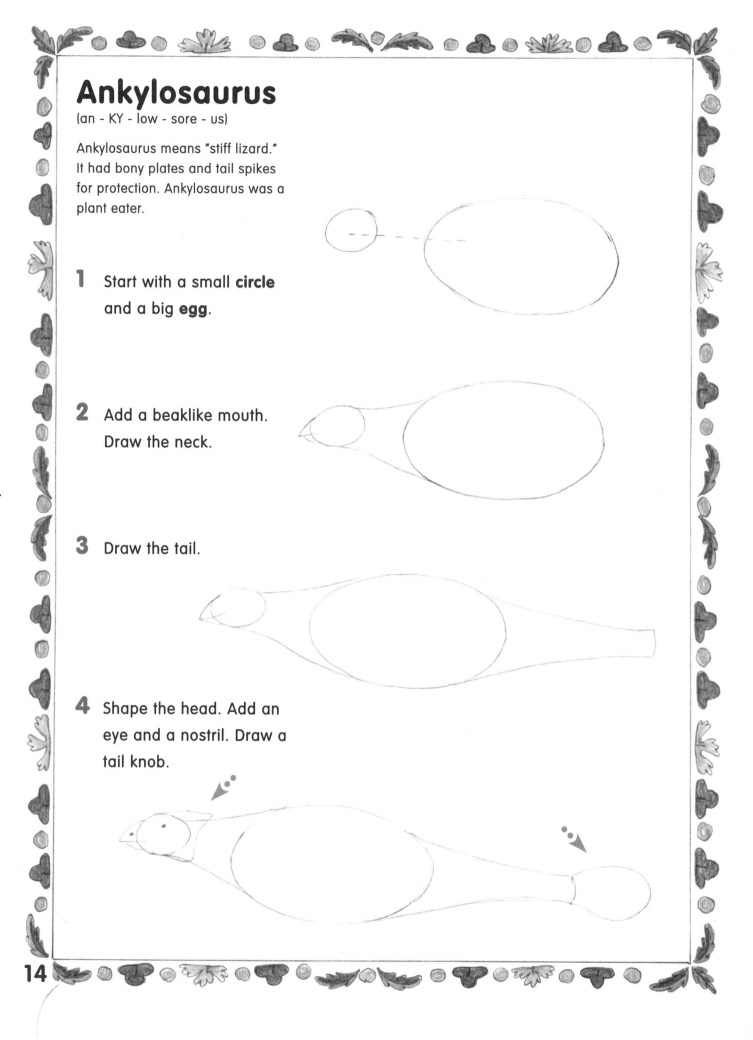

1 Start with a small **circle** and a big **egg**.

2 Add a beaklike mouth. Draw the neck.

3 Draw the tail.

4 Shape the head. Add an eye and a nostril. Draw a tail knob.

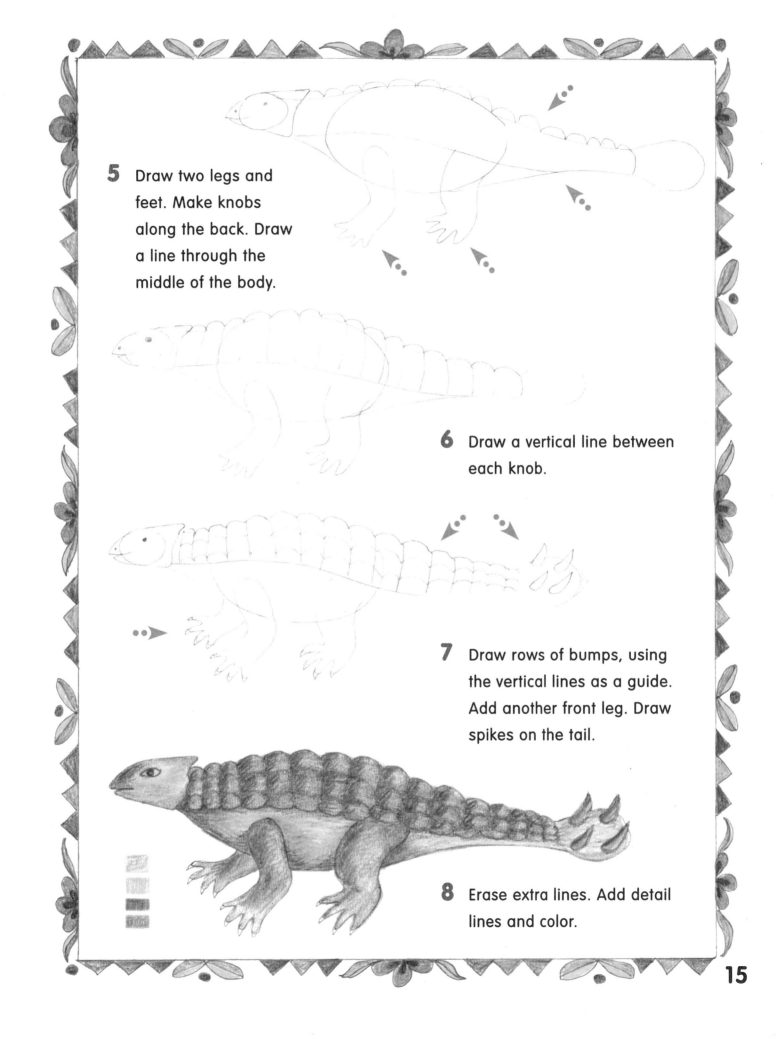

5 Draw two legs and feet. Make knobs along the back. Draw a line through the middle of the body.

6 Draw a vertical line between each knob.

7 Draw rows of bumps, using the vertical lines as a guide. Add another front leg. Draw spikes on the tail.

8 Erase extra lines. Add detail lines and color.

Gallimimus

(Gal - i -MIME - us)

Gallimimus means "like a chicken." Its toothless beak and three-toed feet were bird-like, but it had arms instead of wings. Gallimimus was 17 feet tall, a fast runner and a plant eater.

1 Start with a small **circle** and a big **egg**.

2 Draw a curved, pointy beak and the eye. Draw the neck. Add a long pointy tail.

3 Draw an arm. Draw a leg, in two sections. Add a foot.

16

4 Draw a second leg, in two sections. Add a foot. Draw a second arm.

5 Add claws.

6 Erase extra lines. Add shading and color.

Great Gallimimus!

Diplodocus

(Dih - PLOD - uh - kuss)

Diplodocus means "double beam," which refers to the shape of its backbone. Diplodocus was a 90-foot-long plant eater. It had nostrils on top of its head so that it could be almost totally submerged in water.

1 Start with a tiny **egg** and a big **oval**.

2 Draw a long curved neck. Shape the face and add an eye.

3 Add two legs.

4 Add two more legs.
Draw a long,
snakelike tail.

5 Erase extra lines.
Add shading and color.

Delightful Diplodocus!

Parasaurolophus

(par - ah - sore - OL - uh - fuss)

Parasaurolophus was a member of the duck-billed dinosaur family. Lambeosaurus was its cousin (see page 36). The tube on its head was hollow and connected to its nostrils. It is believed that Parasaurolophus could make loud bellowing noises through its horn. It was a forest dweller who ate mostly leaves, seeds, and twigs.

1 Start with a **circle** and an **oval**.

2 Draw the face. Add an eye. Draw the neck lines. Add a front leg. Draw a rear leg.

3 Add a horn. Make a circle around the eye. Add the nostrils. Add another front and back leg.

Some Parasaurolophus had horns that were six feet long!

4 Add claws.

5 Erase extra lines. Add shading and color.

21

Pachycephalosaurus

(pake - ee - sef - uh - lo -SORE - us)

Pachycephalosaurus was a "bone-head" dinosaur. The top of its skull was twenty times thicker than a person's. It was a lot like having a bowling ball on your head. It may have been used in rivalries or to butt enemies. Pachycephalosaurus, 15 feet tall, had a very hard head and a very small brain.

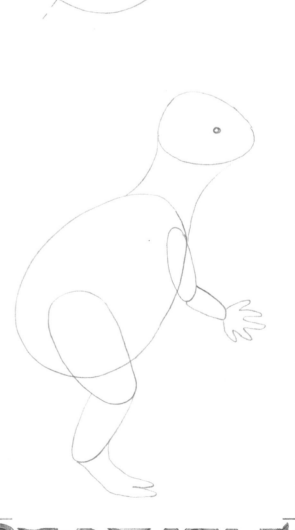

1 Start with two **eggs**. Notice the angles.

2 Add an eye. Draw a curved neck.

3 Add a front leg and a back leg in three sections.

4 Draw the nose. Add a bump to the top of the head. Draw another front and rear leg.

5 Draw bumps on the head and nose. Add the curved tail.

6 Erase extra lines. Add shading and color.

Psittacosaurus

(sih - tak - ah - SORE - us)

Psittacosaurus means "like a parrot," because it had a jaw shaped like a beak. It was a cousin to Triceratops (see page 35). Only five feet tall, Psittacosaurus was a plant eater that walked on all fours.

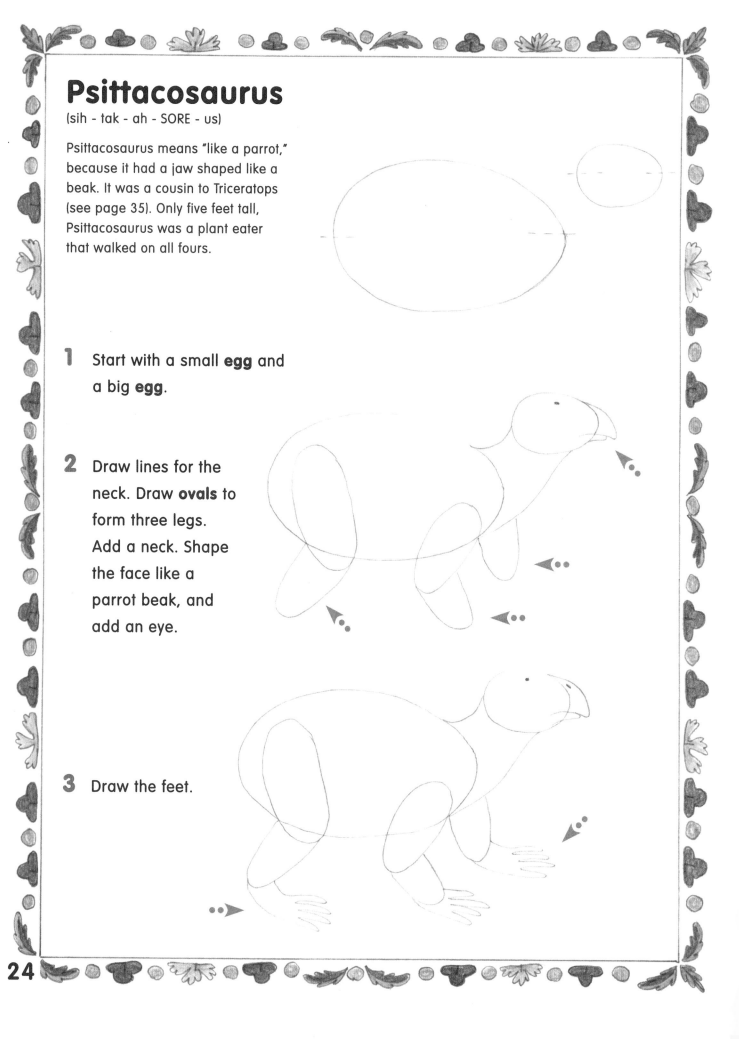

1 Start with a small **egg** and a big **egg**.

2 Draw lines for the neck. Draw **ovals** to form three legs. Add a neck. Shape the face like a parrot beak, and add an eye.

3 Draw the feet.

4 Draw a curving tail.

5 Erase extra lines. Add shading and color.

Pretty Psittacosaurus!

Velociraptor
(Vuh - LOSS - ih - raptor)

Velociraptor means "speedy thief." Only 6 feet tall, this meat eater had sharp eyesight. Velociraptor may have hunted in dim light or at night.

1 Start with an **egg** and a long **oval**.

2 Draw the neck. Shape the face and jaw. Add an eye and nostril. Draw the shapes of the front and back legs.

3 Add claws. Erase extra lines. Add shading and color.

1 Start with an **oval** and an **egg**. Notice the angles.

2 Draw the neck, head and beak. Add the eye.

3 Draw two "arms" with extra long finger bones. Add two legs.

Pteranodon
(ter - AN - o -don)

Pteranodon means "winged and toothless" and was more of a glider than a flier. It was the size of a turkey and ate fish.

4 Attach wings to finger bones. Erase extra lines. Shade and color.

Archaeopteryx

(ar - kay - OP - ter - icks)

Archeopteryx means "ancient wings." One of the first birds, it was the size of a crow. It had feathers and bones like a bird, but it also had claws, teeth, and a long bony tail like a dinosaur.

1 Start with a **circle** and an **egg**.

2 Draw the neck. Draw an eye and a beak. Looking carefully at the example, draw two wings. Add a long tail.

3 Draw lines in wings and widen the tail. Add claws to the wings. Draw teeth. Draw legs and feet.

5 Draw feathers on the wings. Use the curved line you drew to guide you in drawing the feather pattern. Add tail feathers.

6 Erase extra lines. Add shading and color.

Spinosaurus

(spy - no - SORE - us)

Spinosaurus means "spiny lizard." The sail on its back could open like a fan and probably was used as a heat regulator. Meat-eating spinosaurus had teeth as sharp and serrated as steak knives.

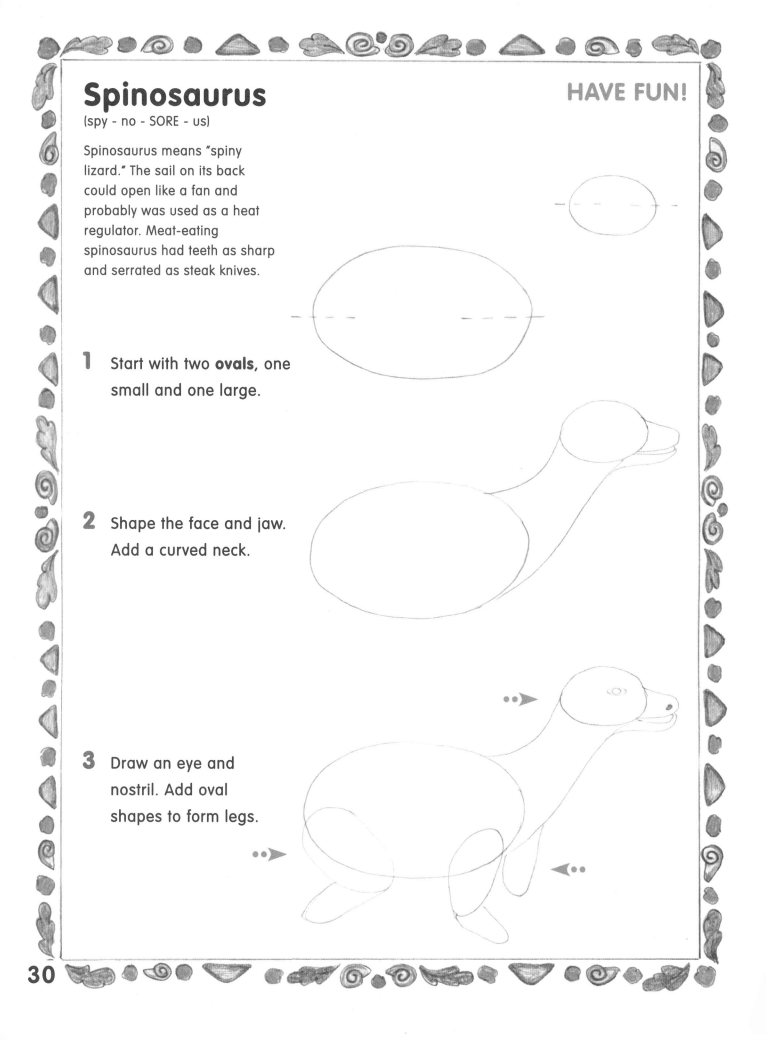

1 Start with two **ovals**, one small and one large.

2 Shape the face and jaw. Add a curved neck.

3 Draw an eye and nostril. Add oval shapes to form legs.

30

4 Finish the eye. Add teeth. Add the other back leg. Draw feet. Add the tail. Draw the back sail.

5 Add vertical lines to the back sail. Erase extra lines. Add shading and color.

Super Spinosaurus!

Ichthyosaurus

(ick - thee - oh - SORE - us)

Ichthyosaurus was not a true dinosaur but a marine reptile. About 6 feet long and a good swimmer, Ichthyosaurus gave birth to live young.

1 Start with an **oval** and a **circle**. Draw the neck and head, and add an eye.

2 Draw the tail. Add a dorsal fin.

3 Add flippers and teeth.

4 Erase extra lines. Add shading and color.

Elasmosaurus

(ee - LAZ - MO - SOR - US)

Elasmosaurus was a swimming reptile. Its long snaky neck was as long as its body. Elasmosaurus had strong jaws and sharp teeth, and ate fish.

1 Start with a small **oval** and a big **oval**.

2 Connect ovals with two long snaky neck lines. Draw a pointy nose. Add an eye.

3 Add the mouth. Draw two flippers. Add two more flippers and a tail.

4 Erase extra lines, and add shading and color.

Compsognathus

(komp - so - NAY - thus)

Compsognathus means "pretty jaw." With hollow bones and birdlike feet, it was the size of a chicken. Fast and agile, compsognathus ate small mammals and lizards.

1 Start with a small **oval** and a larger **oval**. Notice how far apart they are.

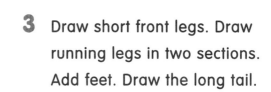

2 Draw a beak, eye, and long curved neck.

3 Draw short front legs. Draw running legs in two sections. Add feet. Draw the long tail.

4 Erase extra lines. Add shading and color.

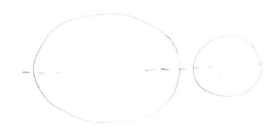

Triceratops
(try - SER - a - tops)

Triceratops' name means "three horns." A 30-foot-long, 6-ton plant eater, its horns were for protection and fighting other Triceratop rivals.

1 Start with an **oval** and a **circle**.

2 Shape the head and add the beaklike mouth. Add an eye. Add a curved tail. Draw two legs.

3 Draw three horns. Add another back leg. Draw another front leg.

4 Erase extra lines. Add shading and color.

Terrific Triceratops!

Lambeosaurus

(lam - bee - oh - SORE - us)

Lambeosaurus was named after Canadian fossil hunter Lawrence Lambe. It was a duck-billed dinosaur related to Parasaurolophus (see page 20). The bony crest had nostrils in it, and may have been used to make sounds and for recognizing individuals. Lambeosaurus was 30 to 50 feet long.

1 Start with a small **egg** and a large **oval**.

2 Add the odd-shaped head bone. Shape the face and jaw. Add nostril and eye. Draw the curving neck.

3 Draw ovals to shape the two front legs and one back leg.

4 Draw front and back feet, with toe nails. Add a curving tail.

5 Erase extra lines. Add shading and color.

Kentrosaurus

(ken - tro - SORE - us)

Kentrosaurus means "spiked lizard."
It was a cousin of Stegosaurus (see
page 10). Tiny brained and toothless,
Kentrosaurus was a plant eater that
walked on all fours. It probably lived
in herds and weighed up to 17 tons.

DRAW LIGHTLY!

1 Start with a tiny **circle**
and a big **egg**.

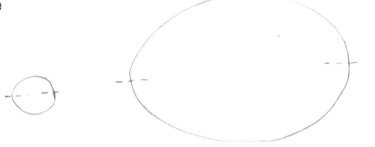

2 Draw the neck by connecting the
two ovals. Shape the face and jaw.
Add a nostril, mouth and eye.

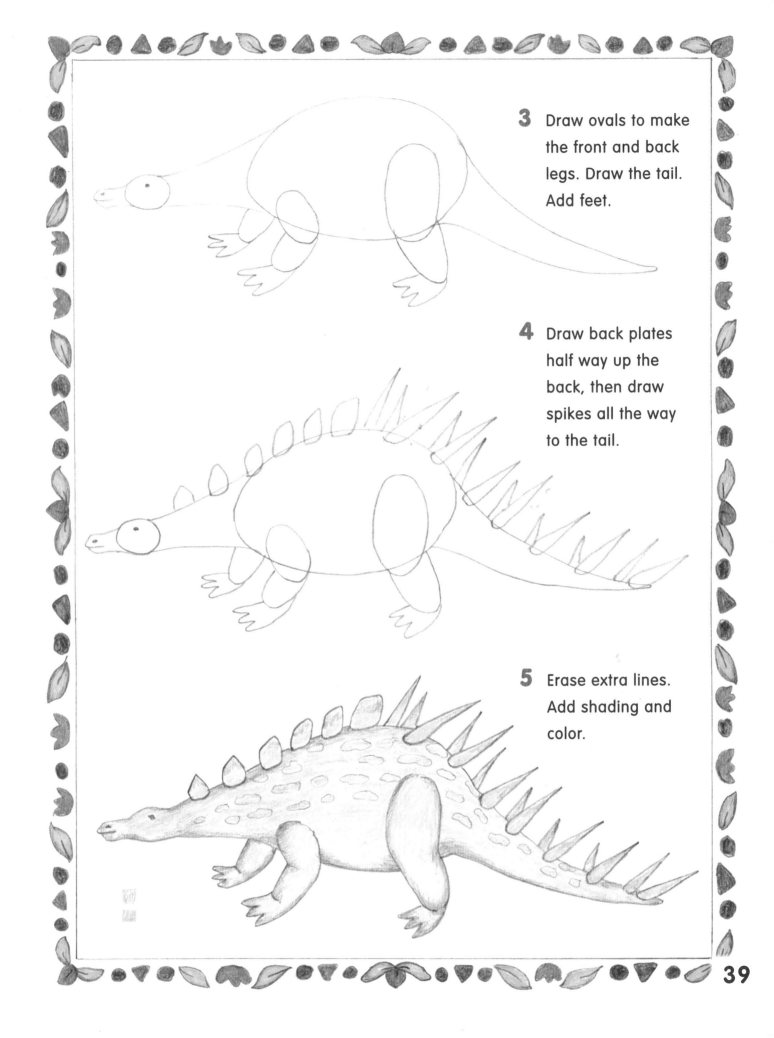

3 Draw ovals to make the front and back legs. Draw the tail. Add feet.

4 Draw back plates half way up the back, then draw spikes all the way to the tail.

5 Erase extra lines. Add shading and color.

Maiasaurus

(My - ah - SORE - us)

Maiasaurus means "good mother lizard." One of the duck-billed dinosaurs, it was about 30 feet long and a plant eater. At a Montana site, fossil hunters discovered an area that contained almost 40 nests, 6 feet across and dug out of the ground. Maiasaurus was indeed a good mother who nurtured her foot-long babies.

1 Start with a big **egg** and a small **egg**.

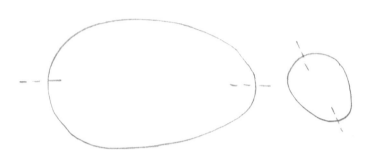

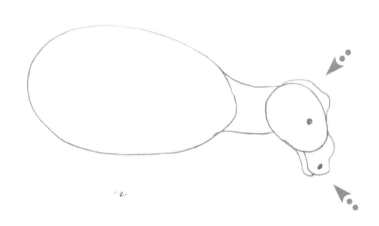

2 Draw a neck. Add a bump on the head. Shape the nose and jaw. Add an eye and nostril.

3 Draw ovals to make four legs.

4 Add four feet and claws. Draw a tail.

5 Erase extra lines. Add shading and color.

Marvelous Maiasaurus!

Morganucodon

(mor - guh - NUKE - uh - don)

Morganucodon was a tiny mammal that lived alongside dinosaurs. It survived by being active at night and eating insects, seeds, and eggs. After dinosaurs disappeared, around 65 million years ago, mammals like Morganucodon took over and began evolving in many different ways.

1 Draw a small **circle** and an **egg**.

2 Shape face and jaw. Draw the neck. Make a circle for the back leg. Draw the front leg and paw. Make a dot for the eye.

3 Add whiskers. Draw an ear. Add another front leg. Draw a long tail.

4 Erase extra lines. Add shading and color.

Hyracotherium

(hy - rak - uh - THEE - r ee - um)
Sometimes called Eohippus
(ee - oh - HIP - us)

Hyracotherium, or Eohippus as it is sometimes called, was an early ancestor of the horse. A tiny fox-sized mammal, it dwelt in forests and ate tender plants.

1 Start with an **oval** and a small **egg**. Notice the angles.

2 Draw the neck. Add an ear, eye, nostril, and mouth.

3 Draw a back leg, front leg, and feet.

4 Draw a mane. Add a tail. Draw some spots. Draw the other legs and feet.

5 Add shading and color.

Hyracotherium had toes on its feet instead of hooves. The name Eohippus means "Dawn horse."

Diatryma

(die - ah - TRY - ma)

Diatryma was a flightless bird, a 7-foot meat-eating terror. It was a forest dweller and probably nested on the ground.

1 Start with a big **circle** and a small **circle**.

2 Draw the neck. Add an eye. Draw tail feathers.

3 Draw an upper beak and lower beak. Begin two legs.

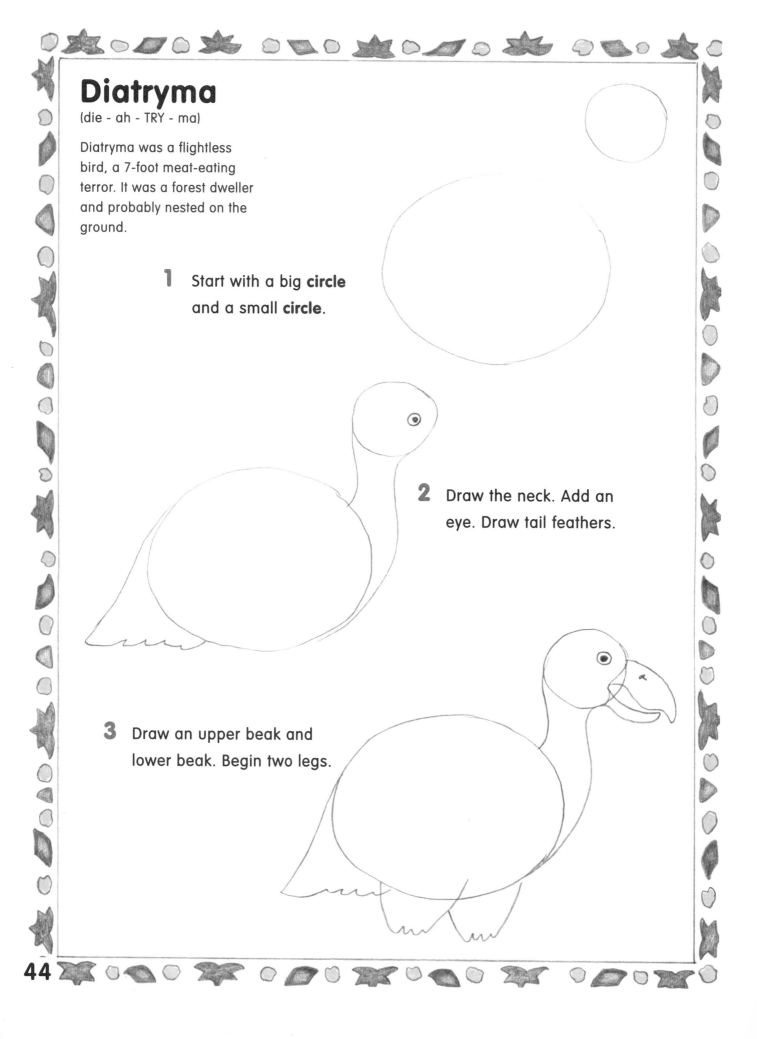

HAVE FUN!

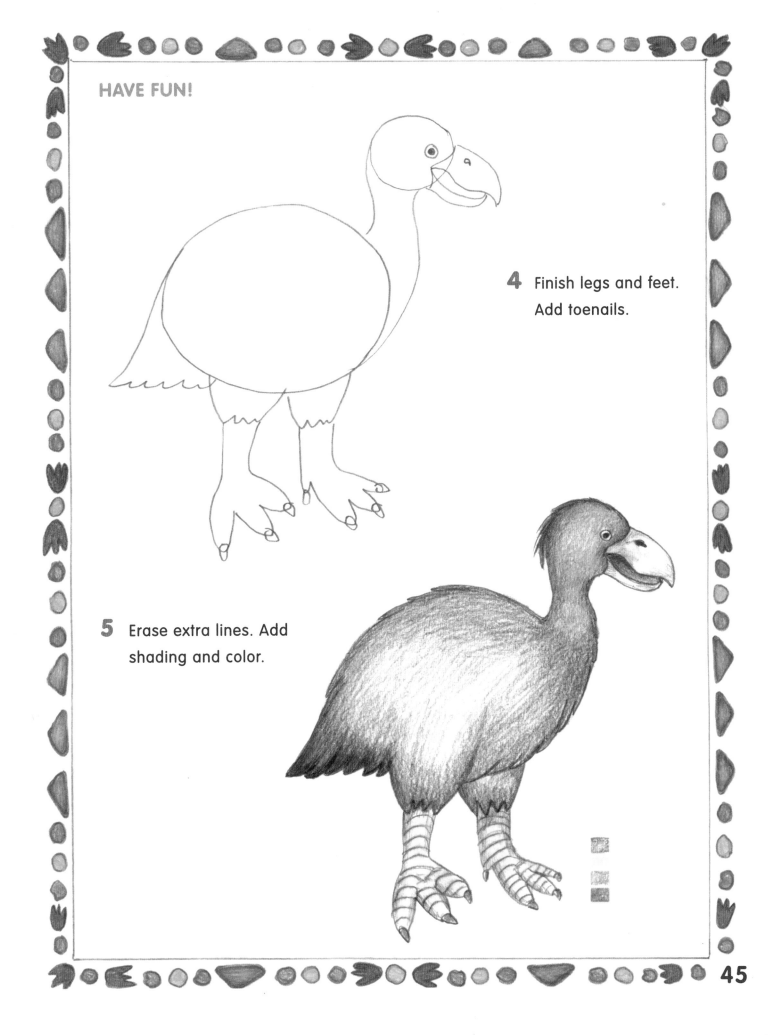

4 Finish legs and feet. Add toenails.

5 Erase extra lines. Add shading and color.

Glyptodon

(GLIP - toe - don)

Glyptodon was a car-sized cousin of the modern armadillo. It was 14 feet long and 5 feet high. It had bony armor on its back and a bony helmet on its head.

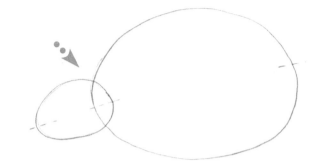

1 Draw a large **oval**. Draw a small **egg** and overlap the **oval**.

2 Add an **oval** on top of head. Make an eye and nose. Draw two legs.

3 Add ears. Draw lines for armor on the head and body. Add a tail with spikes on the end. Draw toenails.

4 Erase extra lines. Add shading and color.

Woolly Mammoth

(MAM - uth)

The Woolly Mammoth was an Ice-Age mammal (see chart on page 62) that was related to the modern elephant. It lived on the edge of glaciers. Its tusks were up to 16 feet long. Whole mammoths have been found preserved in ice in Alaska and Siberia. From this, we know they had shaggy reddish-brown fur.

1 Draw three **eggs**. The big one is in the middle. Notice the angle of all the **eggs**.

2 Draw a line for the head, neck and back. Add an eye. Draw the trunk and mouth.

3 Draw a long curved tusk.
Draw two legs.

4 Draw a second curving
tusk behind the first.
Add toenails.

5 Draw the tail. Add another front and back leg. Draw zigzag lines on the belly for hair.

6 Erase extra lines. Shade and color your Woolly Mammoth. Make it shaggy!

Brontotherium

(BRON - toe - THEE - ree - um)

Brontotherium means "thunder beast." It weighed 5 tons and was 8 feet high. The two horns on its nose may have been used for fighting rivals during mating season.

1 Draw three **eggs**— a medium, a large, and a small one. Notice the angles.

2 Draw a curved line to connect the ovals on top and bottom. Draw an eye and a nostril.

3 Draw two horns. Draw a front leg. Draw a back leg.

4 Draw an ear. Shape the mouth. Draw a tail. Add two more legs. Draw toenails.

5 Erase extra lines. Add shading and color.

Megatherium

(meg - ah - THEE - ree - um)

Megatherium was a giant ground sloth. It was a slow-moving relative of today's tree sloth. About the size of an elephant, Megatherium had bony protective plates under its fur. It died out about 10,000 years ago.

1 Start with a big **egg** and a small **egg**.

2 Draw the neck. Add the tail.

3 Draw an ear. Add an eye. Shape the face.

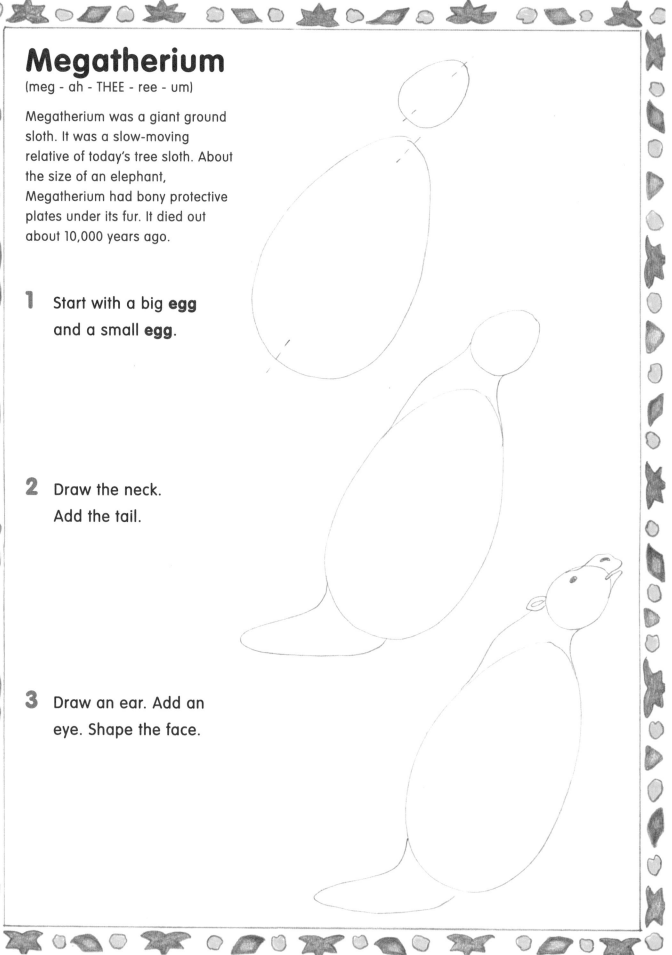

4 Draw two front legs with big curving claws. Draw two back legs with claws.

5 Erase extra lines. Add shading and color.

Smilodon

(SMY - lo - don)

Smilodon is also known as a "saber toothed tiger." Its fangs were razor sharp and 6 inches long. Smilodon died out about 10,000 years ago. We don't know if it had stripes or spots. So why not make some of both?

1 Draw three **eggs**. The first one is the smallest. Notice the angles.

2 Draw curved lines on the top and bottom to connect the ovals. Shape face and jaw.

3 Add the eye and nose. Draw BIG fangs. Draw a front and back leg. Add the tail.

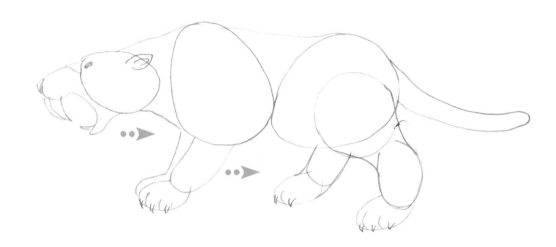

4 Add another fang. Draw another front leg. Draw another back leg. Add claws.

5 Erase extra lines. Add shading, stripes, spots, and coloring.

Super Smilodon!

Megaceros

(mee - GAS - er - us)

Megaceros was also called "Irish Elk."
Many well-preserved specimens were
found in peat bogs in Ireland.
Megaceros died out a few thousand
years ago. It had a 12-foot antler span.

1 Start with a small **egg**
and a big **egg**.

2 Draw a curved neck.
Draw a straight front
leg, and a back leg
in two sections.

3 Draw an eye. Add an
ear. Draw another front
and back leg.

4 Draw his fancy 12-foot antlers. Add hooves. Draw a tail.

5 Erase extra lines. Add shading and color.

Baluchitherium

(ba - LUKE - uh - thee - ree - um)

Baluchitherium was just gigantic. It was the largest land mammal that ever lived. It weighed 20 tons—equal to five elephants. It's related to the modern-day rhinoceros. It ate leaves and twigs—a lot of them!

The name Baluchitherium comes from the old name of the country Pakistan. It was called Baluchistan and that was where this fossil was found in 1911.

1 Draw a VERY big **circle** and a small **oval**.

2 Draw the neck. Add two ears. Shape the face. Draw an eye. Draw a back and front leg.

3 Add a nose and mouth.
Draw another front leg.
Draw another back leg.
Add toenails. Draw the tail.

This diagram shows how big
Baluchitherium was compared
with a modern-day elephant.

4 Erase extra lines. Add
shading and color.

Create Your Own Dinosaurs

These creatures are so fantastic and strange. It would be fun to make up your own dinosaurs and give them a crazy name.

Here are some ideas. What do you think they ate? Where did they live?

shortodon

bizarrosaurus

Drawings on these pages by Daniel Levin.

Draw an environment for your dinosaur!

Polkasaurus?

Time Line
When did they live?

Mezosoic Era:

Triassic period:
Morganucodon

Jurassic period:
Stegosaurus
Diplodocus
Kentrosaurus
Archaeopteryx
Compsognathus
Ichthyosaurus

Cretaceous:
Deinonychus
Triceratops
Tyrannosaurus
Maiasaurus
Iguanodon
Pachycephalosaurus
Spinosaurus
Lambeosaurus
Psittacosaurus
Velociraptor
Ankylosaurus
Pteranodon
Gallimimus
Elasmosaurus
Parasaurolophus

Cenozoic Era:

Ecocene:
Hyracotherium (Eohippus)
Diatryma

Oligocene:
Baluchitherium
Brontotherium

Pleistocene:
Megatherium
Smilodon
Megaceros
Glyptodon
Woolly Mammoth

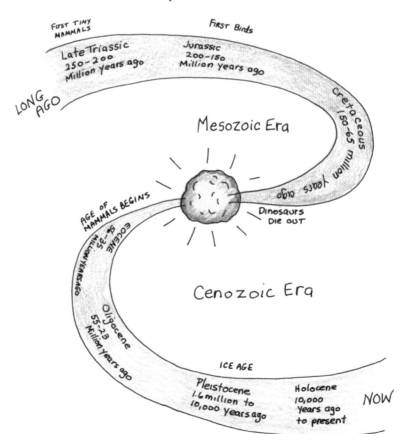

Good Bye Dinosaurs, Hello Mammals

Dinosaurs ruled the Earth for 160 million years. They died out on every continent around 60 million years ago. Scientists believe that a giant meteor crashed into the area that is now Central America. The dust and debris from this event clouded the sun and caused climate changes. The dinosaurs could not adapt to the changes and in a fairly short amount of time, they all disappeared.

Mammals were not affected the same way. The first mammals appeared during the late Triassic period. They were little shrew-like creatures. They were active at night and ate leaves and insects. When the dinosaurs were gone, they emerged from hiding. Soon, they took over in the lands that the dinosaurs had left empty.

Birds first appeared on Earth during the Jurassic period. Archaeopteryx had feathers and wings like a bird, but teeth and claws like meat-eating dinosaurs. Scientists believe that some of the genetic material of the dinosaurs lives on in modern-day birds, their only known surviving relative.

Scientists are learning new things about dinosaurs every day, and so can you!

Index

Learn about other drawing books online at **www.drawbooks.com!**